CW01559146

David Boyle is the author

history, cities, economics

Blondel's Song and *Toward t*   — a fellow

of the New Economics Foundation and lives in Crystal

Palace, next to the Spa Hill Allotments.

www.david-boyle.co.uk

On the Eighth Day,

God Created Allotments

A short history of the allotments movement

David Boyle

THE REAL PRESS
and Endeavour Press
www.endeavourpress.com
www.therealpress.com

First published in 2012 as an ebook by Endeavour Press

www.endeavourpress.com

This printed edition by the Real Press,

The Red House, 56 Dale Park Road, London SE19 3TY

www.therealpress.com

ISBN 978 0 9552263 2 8

Printed in England by think ink, 11-13 Philip Road, Ipswich,

Suffolk, IB2 8BH

To the members
of Spa Hill Allotments Society

I

"The Saxon is not like us Normans. His manners are not so polite.
But he never means anything serious till he talks about justice and
*   right.*
When he stands like an ox in the furrow – with his sullen set eyes on
*   your own,*
And grumbles, 'This isn't fair dealing', my son, leave the Saxon
*   alone."*
Rudyard Kipling, 'Normans and Saxons'

It was one of the biggest rural demonstrations that anyone had seen in England since the Peasants' Revolt. The crowd that squeezed into the centre of Leamington Spa on Good Friday 1872 was largely dressed in smocks and the distinctive fustian jackets of agricultural labourers. Those who were there never forgot it, but few of them realised at the time that it would lead to an extraordinary political campaign – not just for fair wages – but eventually for the chance for people to have a small plot of land they could use to grow their food.

The allotments movement has become an increasingly popular element of life in Britain since then. It stretches back in some ways directly to the medieval

1

commons, where ordinary people could use land to graze a cow or provide themselves with basic necessities. It certainly didn't begin that day in Leamington, but the demonstration launched the political career of one campaigner in particular who was to make the allotments idea central to his political life.

It is nearly a century and a half since Jesse Collings began his bid for 'three acres and a cow' for anyone who wanted them. Even at the time, when the campaign reached its height in the 1880s, it seemed politically impossible to provide that amount of land to everyone. There have been bursts of enthusiasm for similar ideas in the century that followed, perhaps not for acres and cows – but for a small strip of land to grow vegetables, to feed the family or the get closer to nature. Within living memory, the allotments movement – distinctively English, though not confined to England – has been written off completely. Now the demand for a small patch of land is suddenly unquenchable.

How did we get here? To find out, and to start the roller coaster which is the politics of allotments, we need to go back to that afternoon in Leamington in 1872, two months after the original meeting of the Warwickshire farm workers in the nearby village of Wellesbourne. When a group of labourers form Weston-under-

Wetherley had written a letter to the local press asking for their pay to go up to two shillings and sixpence a day, a Primitive Methodist preacher called Joseph Arch had found himself the focus of a growing movement. In February, Arch had stood on a pig stool underneath a chestnut tree in Wellesbourne and launched his campaign. A week later, expecting about 30 in the Stag's Head in the same village, Arch found that 2,000 farm workers had turned out to hear him on a cold, wet, night, holding flickering lanterns on bean poles.

In the two months since then, a great deal had happened. The treatment of farm labourers had become a national debate. The farmers, the squirearchy and the Church of England clergy had bitterly opposed the labourers on the issue. Wellesbourne landowner Sir Charles Mordaunt was even evicting any of his tenants who joined the union. Tempers were high. Now, in Leamington on Good Friday, the first item in the packed meeting was to decide on a name for the new, and unique, organisation of farm workers, and they decided with little fuss that it would be called the Warwickshire Agricultural Labourers' Union. Next was to decide the terms of their demands to the farmers, and they set the minimum weekly wage at 16 shillings, and the limit to the working day at ten hours – with a 4pm end on Saturdays.

It was a thrilling moment. Here was a gathering of the truly dispossessed, all those dismissed as know-nothing yokels in the genteel pavements of Leamington, setting out their demands in their country speech – it was a vision of the world turned upside down. Once the hall was filled, there were still crowds trying to get in. An impromptu open air meeting was organised with the *Daily News* war correspondent Archibald Forbes in the chair. He had made his reputation writing about the Paris Commune the previous year and been sent up from London to cover the emerging agricultural clash.

Inside the main meeting, it was announced that a 'friend' in Birmingham was donating £100 to the cause. It was widely understood that this had probably come from the man who would make his national reputation the following year as the first Liberal Mayor of Birmingham, screw manufacturer Joseph Chamberlain, who would soon be recognisable by crowds across the country, with his orchid in his buttonhole and his monocle perched in his eye socket, as 'Radical Joe'.

The fact that people like Chamberlain in nearby Birmingham were backing the cause was a huge boost to the farm workers, but the key moment that evening in Leamington was the speech by Chamberlain's lifelong friend and ally Jesse Collings, who was to become the key figure in the allotments movement in Britain, and who is the key figure in this book.

Collings was instantly recognisable, because his huge side whiskers somehow marked him out as rural. He was then forty years old, the youngest of eleven children of a self-employed bricklayer from Littleham, outside Exmouth in Devon, born on 2 December 1831. He rose to be a privy councillor and a respected member of the Liberal establishment, but he never forgot that he was born into a family of peasant proprietors. That was what brought him out of Birmingham that afternoon – probably with news of Chamberlain's donation in his pocket. He may have been the proprietor of Collings & Wallis Ltd, selling household goods made in the Birmingham factories – having started out as a journeying salesman, but he grew up with an allotment:

"When my father began business for himself, he rented four acres of land, two acres of which were attached to the new house he had built for himself and two acres a short distance away. On these four acres we grew wheat, barley, potatoes, and other vegetables. We kept a number of pigs and a large number of fowls. For myself I had a fancy for rabbits, guinea-pigs, hedgehogs, and ferrets. We grew each year sufficient wheat to supply the family with bread."[1]

This memory was central to Collings' political life, partly because he adored his father, and partly because of his memories of agricultural poverty that he had witnessed as a salesman wandering twice a year across a beat that covered the whole of western England. Collings was always proud of the achievements of that peasant class, and aware how much they had been dragged down to subsistence level, by poor pay but also because their access to the land had been seriously curtailed. They could no longer grow their own food.

Collings talked about the vital importance of a stake in the land for the poor as well as the rich landowners. He was duly elected onto the finance committee of the new union. Sine weeks later, at the second national rally, he rose to commit himself to the farm workers' cause, and – as he did so – a small piece of paper was passed along the table of dignitaries until it reached him. It was a telegram, which read: "Return at once. Your warehouse is on fire." He crumpled the paper in his hand, finished the speech and hurried back to Birmingham.

---

[1] Jesse Collings and Sir John L. Green (1920) *Life of the Rt Hon Jesse Collings*, Longmans, Green, London, 1.

These two rallies provided a launch for what rapidly became a nationwide strike, followed shortly afterwards by a lock-out by the farmers. The landowners had assumed that the struggle would last a week, but Archibald Forbes made an immediate impression on public opinion with his *Daily News* articles, and support and cheques were soon pouring in. By the end of the lock-out, the union was national, it had recruited 50,000 members, and most of the farmers had succumbed and raised the wages as requested.

But it was a painful and divisive process. Clergymen had their church bells rung to drown out the village meetings by striking farm workers. People were sacked from church choirs for their involvement in the union, or evicted from their church allotments, often the only way they managed to keep themselves alive through the winter, strikes or no strikes. In Chipping Norton in Oxfordshire, two magistrates sentenced sixteen local women to ten days imprisonment with hard labour, for threatening strike breakers from taking their husband's jobs. Troops had to be called out to prevent a riot as the women were driven to Oxford Prison. Worse, once the harvest was over, the wages went down again.

Meanwhile the union funds were being used up at a tremendous rate, subsidising the emigration to Canada of labourers who had lost jobs or tenancies as a result of their union activities. Accusations of embezzlement were encouraged by their political opponents. The campaign began to falter.

Collings' interest also began to shift. His friend Chamberlain was now preparing to take political control of Birmingham, which was then a stinking hellhole of raw sewage and poverty presided over by a group of friends who met weekly in a pub called the Woodman, and prided themselves on how little they spent. They called themselves 'The Economists'. By the end of 1873, Chamberlain would be Mayor and Collings would be chairing his Libraries and Art Gallery Committee, organising free concerts for working people.

But there was another problem. Collings was certainly committed to the farm worker's cause, but his main interest was in reviving the idea of agriculture itself, both for rural communities and for the urban poor. Throughout the divisive strike, and the years that followed, he tried desperately, but unsuccessfully, to keep open communications with the farmers as well. More important still than the struggle for fair wages for agricultural workers was the struggle to reverse those forces that were driving people off the land.

Collings was born into the generation that had begun to glimpse the possibilities of technology in the fields. High pressure boilers appeared in the 1850s, which made the traction engines lighter. The phrase 'portable machinery' began appearing in the farming world. The repeal of the Corn Laws may have reduced the price of bread, but it had also introduced a flood of cheap foreign imported grain which undercut the produce from British farms, especially from the USA now that the Civil War was over.

Bad harvests, foot and mouth outbreaks and liver rot, all combined to make things worse. In the 1870s alone, the urban population of Britain rose by a quarter, as farm workers left the land in their hundreds of thousands. Over the next three decades, wheat acreage in England fell by half, and the new steam-driven machinery meant that, despite the exodus from the land, there still wasn't enough work to go around. It was hardly surprising that the influx of labourers was accelerating from the countryside to an uncertain, and often poverty stricken, future in cities like Birmingham.

The conventional solution was not higher wages; it was emigration to the colonies, by force if necessary. This was hardly a new idea, but Collings fought this with all the energy he could muster, because he saw where it would lead – an empty, useless British countryside while cities ate imported food. The problem was not that there were too many people tilling the land, he said, it was that there were far too few.

But his argument was broader. It was about re-establishing a closer connection with the land, in cities and countryside. No victory by farm labourers at the expense of the farmers would achieve that. Somehow it required an alliance between both sides to raise the profile of agriculture in a nation that was beginning to think it was old-fashioned and unnecessary. So when Collings was asked to stand for Parliament in Ipswich in 1880, it was the cause of land reform that convinced him that he had to try. The real problem was that most of the population of the countryside had no property and therefore could not vote. It was hardly surprising that the decision-making of the nation was so unbalanced. There could be no real solution without their votes.

As a backbench Liberal MP, there was little Collings could do by himself to widen the rural franchise, but there was a cause he could work at. Collings believed that agricultural families – whether they were in poverty or just on strike – would be considerably less dependent on events, less forced to accept the lowest wage, if they had a small piece of land they could call their own. Yet over the past seven years of the farm workers' battle, he had seen how these allotments could be removed from their tenants on a whim, or because the church elders disapproved of the tenants. Worse, sometimes just because the local charity trustees just sat on the money and let the land lie idle.

Here was a cause he could devote his parliamentary career to, and the forces were gathering in the 1880s that would give him an opportunity to do so. Radical thought was beginning to assign the land a romantic, mystical and democratic quality, which challenged its narrow ownership. "God gave the land to the people," went the Liberal Party song in the 1880s. As far as Collings was concerned, if God gave the land, then he gave the allotments too.

II

"Spirits that call and no one answers -
Ha'nacker's down and England's done.
Wind and Thistle for pipe and dancers,
And never a ploughman under the sun:
Never a ploughman. Never a one."
Hilaire Belloc, 'Ha'nacker Mill'

Collings may not have known it, but when he took his seat in Parliament, his sprouting cheeks marking him out as a countryman among the well-heeled frock coats and top hats, but he was about to articulate a very old tradition of radicalism indeed.

The idea that life would be simpler, and more peaceful and congenial, if it was rooted in the land and changing seasons, goes back to Hesiod and Virgil. The agrarian tradition in poetry and painting, as in politics, was defiantly anti-modern, just as it was defiantly anti-money. It went hand in hand with a political tradition that regards the cities as the source of corruption and money as the source of distorted values. Perhaps this is hardly surprising, because the invention of money was the very phenomenon that made cities possible. It meant those with the power could take their rents with them – or get them sent on – to urban palaces which sucked out the hard won, hard grown, wealth from the countryside they left behind. Here, in the very invention of portable wealth, lies the heart of the complaint, and it made possible a tradition that denies that real wealth lies anywhere but in the soil, in the relationship of humanity to the changing seasons and from there to the infinite.

This is a peculiar political ideology, sometimes completely underground, sometimes purely literary. But it is also deeply nostalgic, looking backwards – not just to a better balance between city and country – but to a paradoxical connection between tilling the land and spirituality. In the nineteenth century, it emerged in a distinctive form in England – or, to be precise, in southern England and the Home Counties – as a response to the Industrial Revolution, and the centralisation of political and financial power in the capital city. It was a response as much to the sheer greed of the London elite as it was to William Blake's dark satanic mills.

The main theme of this discourse was the enclosures of land, parcelling up the commons for the benefit of local landowners, in the name of more efficient agriculture. You can hear its voice in the yeoman farmer Thomas Foster whose impassioned shout from the choir in Louth in Lincolnshire in October 1536 launched the Pilgrimage of Grace against the selling off of monasteries and monastic land.

Or the Parliamentarian colonel Edward Whalley more than a century later, rolling back enclosures in the face of a new Parliamentary enthusiasm for them, before he fled under the threat of arrest after the Restoration all the way to New England (he was said to have lived there in a cave).

Or Peter Chamberlain, surgeon and Anabaptist after the English Civil War, whose proposal for a national bank to lend money to the poor to cultivate waste land and forests never happened – perhaps because of his accompanying proposal to use the nation's palaces as agricultural communes.

Or Gerald Winstanley, the digger leader, struggling to make the earth a 'Common Treasury' at St George's Hill, Weybridge.

Or another century after that, you can hear the same voice from the agricultural reformer Arthur Young when he changed his mind about enclosures, after 46 volumes of his *Annals of Agriculture*, claiming that: "I had rather that all the commons of England were sunk in the sea, than that the poor should in future be treated on enclosing as they have been hitherto."

That is the heart of the Back to the Land tradition: the idea that there are other truths more important than those generally accepted by our rulers. From that idea derives all the rest – the antipathy towards money as a measure of progress, the scepticism towards conventional luxuries and rewards. A return to the simplicity of natural things as the basis for progress. A melancholic sense of a natural, balanced past that needs to be rebuilt, rather than a utopian joy at a radical future that is being invented afresh. But above all, it is a rejection of materialistic values and a striving for something else that is both stubbornly of the world and yet also beyond it.

This is a dangerous tradition of politics, consistently rejecting what is mainstream and conventional. It is fierce and occasionally intolerant. It terrifies the establishment so much that they deny its existence, but it has also become distinctively English, based on traditional English heresy (British medieval heresies were not about purity, as they were on the continent: they were Pelagian. This was a heresy that revelled in the stuff of the world, the plough and the soil, as the source of virtue and simplicity).

Whether or not this was the reason, the English gentry did not pine – as the continental gentry so often did – for urban living. They settled in the countryside themselves. When the countryside rose up against the town, as it did in England too, this was not necessarily the poor against the rich – it was the powerless against the powerful, those who grew vegetables against those who grew money. The records of those punished for their involvement in the Peasant's Revolt includes a number of well-to-do country types, yeomen farmers, clergymen and tradesmen.

When the European romantic movement flowered in the eighteenth century, it developed a nostalgia for the simple life, from Rousseau's Noble Savage to Matthew Arnold's Scholar Gipsy, all people who lived outside cities, but they were not known for what they actually *did*, apart from communing with nature. In England, in particular, it also crystallised around something much older – and more active: nostalgia for English rural village life, for the cycle of peasant work, and the sturdy independence of peasant freeholding – underpinned by half-forgotten common laws dating back to King Alfred and before.

"The poorest man, that sees his maker, and lives in the light, though he could never read a letter in the book," wrote the Digger leader Gerald Winstanley, "dares throw the glove to all the humane learning in the world, and declare the deceit of it."[2]

This was clearly not a Protestant tradition: it refused to demonise nature as the Protestants tended to do. Nor was it really a socialist tradition, except in the most basic sense: it is a non-utopian future based on small scale land ownership, co-operation and common land – and the freedom to grow food. Nor is it really Conservative: the tradition seeks to overturn those who run the world. On the other hand, the Back to the Land tradition seems to have involved people declaring allegiance to nearly every possible political tradition: Radicals (William Cobbett), Tories (John Ruskin, or so he said), Socialists (William Morris), Liberals (Hilaire Belloc, to start with), Greens (Fritz Schumacher), even Blackshirts (Henry Williamson).

These are all literary or artistic figures whose politics has been dismissed as maverick or peculiar because the establishment prefers to pretend that they represent no coherent political tradition. Actually, they do, and the beliefs that hold them together is remarkably consistent:

1.   They look back to a great golden age of agrarian independence and equality, based on the rights to land,

[2] Quoted in Christopher Rowland (2007), *The Cambridge Companion to Liberation Theology*, Cambridge University Press.

swept away in a great Original Sin – whether it was the Norman Conquest, the Enclosures, the Dissolution of the Monasteries or the Industrial Revolution.

2.   They urge a return to those peasant values of thrift and independence, based on a programme borrowing from the best of Medieval economics – whether it is common land, the guild system or the concept of the Just Price.

3.   They share a bitter scepticism about the conventional values of wealth, power and money, and the delusions of money as a measure of value.

4.   They blame the division between rich and poor on urban greed, the manipulation of money, and the theft from the poor of the means of livelihood on the land.

5.   They peddle an alternative interpretation of wealth: that creative human life, lived with work and life in harmony, and close to the seasons, is both spiritual and sacred.

It is also paradoxical. It is a tradition of politics that is so conservative that it is radical. It is deeply romantic, but also practical – it is about putting wasted resources to use. It is also defiantly unconventional. Most of those who have pedalled the politics of Back to the Land through history have been sceptical about conventional education – at least classroom education – and, until the mid-twentieth century, sceptical about feminism. Hilaire Belloc and G. K. Chesterton, who took up Jesse Collings' campaign after he died, were both against widening the franchise to women, though – to provide them with some excuse – this was largely because of their contempt for Parliament rather than their contempt for women.

Jesse Collings shared neither of these scepticisms. Nor did he share Belloc and Morris' contempt for Parliament – William Morris turned Parliament into a dung store in his romance about the future, *News from Nowhere*. But he did share the central objective: to reinvent a peasant tradition in England, providing people with land where they could support, supplement or make their living. That was also the political dream of William Cobbett, shared by the artist Samuel Palmer and his teacher William Blake. It was contemplated by the two great critics of the Victorian age, John Ruskin and William Morris because they imagined a new medieval future, based on craftsmanship, small-scale workshops and a massive return to the land.

None of the conventional political parties ever made serious attempts to represent this lost tradition of English radicalism. Ruskin himself described himself in a whole range of political colours, explaining that the one party he could never support was the Liberals. Morris, Belloc and Chesterton all began as Liberals only to turn their backs on the party in later life – Belloc was even a Liberal MP.

Yet there was then a mismatch between the Back to the Land tradition and the mainstream Liberal Party. It was recognisably agrarian where the party was more industrial. It tended towards high Anglicanism or Catholicism where the party was non-conformist. It was deeply melancholic where the party was hopelessly optimistic. It was interested in the economic roots of liberty when the party was interested in the political roots. And its interest in free trade was always more flexible, and sometimes unrecognisable.

Jesse Collings was a Liberal, though – like his friend Chamberlain – he was always sceptical about the benefits of free trade, and towards the end of his life he was absolutely opposed, afraid that cheap agricultural imports were undermining the economic basis of agriculture back home. In fact, when Collings was consolidating himself in Birmingham and finding a political voice during the 1860s, it must have appeared to be a great age of peasant emancipation. Abraham Lincoln's Emancipation Proclamation in 1863 freed the American slaves and, at a stroke, created a whole new class of peasant proprietors. The trouble was that naivety about economics plunged the freed slaves into an economic slavery known as *peonage*, whereby they owed so much money for their equipment and seeds, and paid so much money for their rent, that they remained enslaved, in effect, often to their previous masters.

A similar situation prevailed in Russia, where the serfs were freed in 1861. Yes, they had been freed from the bonds that controlled their lives – they were free to marry who they wanted, own property and leave their villages – but they had to pay their former masters for their land they used. This was valued at three and a half times the market rate and the serfs, Russia's new peasant proprietors, were expected to pay off the money, which had already been advanced by the government, at 6 per cent interest for 49 years – and did so until the payments were cancelled in 1907.

Anyone like Collings, who was interested in reform – and particularly interested in reform in other countries – realised that a new class of English small landowners, would need more than just rights. They would require access to land to supplement their income and, as far as possible, it would have to be debt free. Then and only then would there be any chance of rebuilding that class of small or part-time farmers that he and Chamberlain encountered so often on their summer tours of the continent together – independent, dignified and proud, with wads of bank notes in their back pockets. That was the objective. It meant dismantling the prevailing pattern of land ownership. It also meant the radical step of introducing similar plots of land into cities to underpin the livelihoods of the urban poor.

Collings also embraced the Back to the Land tradition in the way that explained the extremes of poverty and urban squalor that were all around him in Birmingham. Like Cobbett before him, he blamed the enclosure of land and the destruction of the medieval commons. Like Ruskin and Morris, he blamed the greedy landowners, the intellectual and political heirs of Henry VIII, who had driven peasants off the land to be powerless supplicants to big employers in the cities.

You might not be able to reverse the Industrial Revolution, even if you wanted to. But you could provide poor people with land, even in the cities, which would allow them a small measure of liberty. They need not then choose the lowest wages. They could support themselves at subsistence levels if necessary. They need not be removed to the colonies by do-gooders or end up in the workhouse. For Collings and his friends, allotments were not just a means of providing cheap vegetables. They were a guarantee of liberty.

III

"I discovered at last, that even in all that labyrinth of the new London by night, there is an unvisited hour of almost utter stillness, before the creaking carts begin to come in from the market gardens, to remind us that there is still somewhere a countryside. And in that stillness, I have sometimes fancied I heard, tiny and infinitely far away, something like a faint voice hailing and the sound of horse hoofs that return."

William Cobbett

These were not unfamiliar ideas. The great agrarian radical William Cobbett had written *Cottage Economy* as a guide book to support those few cottagers clinging to the old way of life. The Chartists had included access to land among their demands for a widening of democracy. There were even allotments in many villages, though often – as we have seen – they were often under the control of local busybodies who disapproved of those who might have used them.

Between 1760 and 1801, nearly 1,500 Acts of Parliament, were passed to legalise the enclosures of land, which accelerated to almost one a week. Many of the new laws dealt with ancient 'fuel rights', the local right to gather wood for the fire, and the solution was often to provide land for that purpose. That is the origin of the word which still carries something of a stigma: the land is 'allotted' to the poor. The General Inclosure Act of 1801 formalised this. Whenever land was enclosed, allotments had to be provided next to the poorhouse – when there was one – to grow food which could be sold to support the people living inside.

This was the generation which read Thomas Malthus and shivered in terror at the prospect of a burgeoning and unmanageable poor. The cost of the poor by the 1820s, paid for by the parishes under the Elizabethan Poor Law, was approaching a fifth of national income. There must come a time, said Malthus, when the poor would simply overwhelm the rest. The idea of providing allotments for the workhouses was more to do with tackling rising costs than it was for tackling the root causes of poverty.

Only in 1819, at the height of unemployment from the returning soldiers and seamen of the Napoleonic War – the year of the Peterloo Massacre – some of these workhouse allotments were finally let to people in parishes to try to prevent poverty in the first place. Why force people into the parish relief when they could grow their own, after all? From 1832, the year of the Great Reform Act – with Cobbett finally in Parliament himself –

parish wardens were given the power to break up the old allotments into individual plots.

All these small developments coincided with crisis in social order, and the early 1830s were still echoing with the excitement of the so-called Captain Swing uprisings in southern England. Before the riots, Cobbett had been nearly a lone voice warning about agricultural poverty. His *Rural Rides* had chronicled the plight of so many struggling families living in squalor in the countryside. He had a powerful influence on readers in the labouring classes, but his diagnosis of the problem – poverty ushered in by the enclosure of land – cut little ice with his more powerful contemporaries. When he convinced the parish of Bishop Waltham in Hampshire to debate handing over a small tract of waste land to tenants with families, he was the only one to vote for it. Cobbett was the most formidable campaigner of his era, but he remained infuriatingly out on a limb.

But he also knew the crisis was coming. From May 1829, there were farm workers protesting across the Home Counties. By the following year, there were rick burnings and barn store burnings. Rick burning was rapidly made a hanging offence. Cobbett tiptoed along a legal tightrope, refusing to praise the burnings, but pointing out whenever he could that they were inevitable.

"The history of the whole world contains not one single instance of oppression being put an end to by the humility of the oppressed," he wrote.[3]

The Swing riots came to a head in Cobbett's native north Hampshire at a meeting of his readers at the Swan Inn, Sutton Scotney, where a farm worker called Joseph Mason was delegated to draft a petition for the king. When the signatures had been collected, he set off on foot the 60 miles to find him in Brighton. There he was kept waiting while a letter was drafted explaining that the petition needed to go through the proper channels in Westminster. Mason had too little money to walk on to London, so he gave the petition to a friend who promised to give it to Cobbett.

But the frustration of the petitioners erupted the following month when they began smashing threshing machines. When the local Tory MP and landowner Bingham Baring – a member of the banking family, as Cobbett noted – confronted the marchers, he was hit on the head by an eighteen-year-old ploughman called Henry Cook. Baring was not badly hurt. The next day he responded by gathering a posse together and attacking the farm of one of the wealthier petitioners. He was fined

---

[3] *Political Register* (1825), 19 Feb.

£50 for this act of violence but, for the blow to the head, Henry Cook was hanged.

The Great Reform Act followed two years later, but it was hardly the breakthrough that its advocates assumed. The pace of change was also increasing and the General Enclosure Acts of 1836 and 1840 made it possible for landowners to enclose land without reference to parliament as long as a majority of them (in value and number) agreed to do so. Of the 615,000 acres enclosed under those acts, only around 2,200 acres actually became allotments, but even this measure was becoming controversial. It seemed to the utilitarians to encourage the poor; it seemed to the landowners to get in the way of the natural order of things. "He was tremendously fierce against allotments, and analysed the system with merciless sarcasm," said Benjamin Disraeli's character Lord Marney in his 1845 novel *Sybil*. Others felt the same, yet this kind of provision was still hopelessly inadequate. Even the 'guinea gardens' put on the outskirts of the cities at the end of the eighteenth century were being overwhelmed as the cities burst their boundaries. Cobbett hated the cities, but what happened to the poor when they made their way there, huddled in polluted squalor, was beyond his horizon.

Where Cobbett had glimpsed something important for the future was one of the peculiar observations he made on his Rural Rides. He noticed that the poorer the soil in the countryside, the better off the labourers were. Why should that be? It was because, when the land was poor, labourers were tolerated there and allowed smallholdings which they could look after, and to produce food to underpin their financial security. When the land was rich, it was likely to be enclosed for the benefit of the wealthy landowners, or parcelled up for the benefit of speculators and financiers. Here, hidden away in Cobbett's millions of words, was a key idea that could be put to practical use. Just because marginal land was not as good quality as the rest, it did not mean that it was useless. With intensive attention and care, even waste land could be made productive.

That is what allotments have been ever since. They may not be the world's most fertile soil, or in the most convenient places – quite the reverse. They may not lend themselves to consolidation and industrial scale farming. But give them intensive care, and they will produce. But there is a small miracle behind the idea and, like so much else, Cobbett noticed the phenomenon first. When you lavish care on a small plot of land, however poor quality the soil, it can be much more productive than the same bit of land which is farmed on a bigger scale.

Cobbett first discovered this important truth when he was defending Horton Heath in Dorset from enclosure. "The cottagers produced from their little bits, in food, for themselves, and in things to be sold at market, more than any neighbouring farm of 200 acres," he wrote:

"I learned to hate a system that could induce them to tear up 'wastes'; and keep away occupiers like those I have described. Wastes indeed! Give a dog an ill name. Was Horton Heath waste? Was it waste when a hundred, perhaps, of healthy boys and boys played there on a Sunday, instead of creeping about covered in filth in the alleys of a town."[4]

The vital importance of the land he called 'wastes' was only half the argument here. Cobbett had found that cornucopia of plenty that allotments can represent. It is precisely the opposite to the modern assumption that big intensive monocultural agriculture is more productive

---

[4] John M. Cobbett and James P. Cobbett (eds.) (1855) *Selections from William Cobbett's Political Works*, Anne Cobbett, London, Vol 6, 119.

than small-scale, labour-intensive mixed production. Big scale farming became the ideal of agricultural policy the world over, but – as Cobbett could see in the wastes of Horton Heath two centuries ago – it isn't actually the most productive.

The economist Amartya Sen has since confirmed what he found.[5] It even works in countries like Brazil, where the biggest farmers have grabbed the best land, but again Cobbett had been there first.[6] He noted that ten farms of a hundred acres each could produce more than one farm of a thousand acres. But it was a varied and diverse productivity, compared to the handful of products grown by the big farms. Why? Attention to detail, the personal touch? Nobody has ever quite worked that out, but it remains true today – and not just in farms but in other areas of production as well. The externalities of big scale production very rapidly overwhelm the economies of scale.

This is important for the argument for allotments that was to be wielded by Collings and his allies. Marginal land need not be wasted. The people who had used that

---

[5] Amartya Sen (1962) 'An Aspect of Indian Agriculture', *Economic Weekly*, Vol 14.
[6] Giovanni Cornia (1985) 'Farm Size, Land Yields and the Agricultural Production function: an analysis for 15 Developing Countries', *World Development*, Vol 13, 513-34.

same land as commons in the Middle Ages were not wasted either. There was no need to send their children so brutally to Canada or Australia to be cheap farm hands. It meant that access to the basics of life could be given back to the poor, despite the enclosures. What is more, the land would produce – it could be the source of plenty, because of the close attention it would receive.

This was the central political demand of the Back to the Land movement as it developed towards the end of the Victorian Age. It was romantic about the outdoor life and nature, but not – like the emerging conservation movement – regarding the countryside as a place to be preserved so that the middle classes could ramble about for their weekends. 'Back to the land' meant a way of re-inventing work, giving people more control over it, rather than the whistles of factories, and to provide a source of income. Not just in the rural area either, but to retro-fit agriculture into the cities. That was what Jesse Collings was preparing to do.

IV

"In former times, the agricultural labourer was a man who generally possessed land and almost invariably had rights in common in connection with the cartilage of his cottage. This enabled him to keep stock of various kinds and of more or less value, the proceeds of which, added to his earnings as a labourer, placed him in a fairly prosperous condition. The modern agricultural labourer is a mere wage receiver."
Jesse Collings, *Land Reform*, 1908

Collings was the first of the agricultural workers union leaders to be elected to parliament. He was finally in a position to being pressure to bear on national policy. The objective was to revive English agriculture, but that had to be a long-term aspiration. The Victorian Liberal Party was a largely urban phenomenon, underpinned by the growth of nonconformity. It would require time to shift its attention to the countryside, so he and his allies searched for something which they could do immediately. Collings and the union therefore drew up the first of a series of bills that would give poor people rights over land, to "restore the connection, now almost destroyed, between the cultivator and the soil". If he could get them enacted, he said, it "would largely diminish pauperism;

and would increase the numbers, and raise the social condition of the rural population".[7]

The key reform was for the state to help labourers become their own landlords. It was an idea bitterly opposed by the big landowners, perhaps unsurprisingly, who regarded it as the first stage of a radical expropriation of their inheritance. It was also opposed by the farmers, and much of Collings' campaigning was designed to persuade them it would also benefit them. Cynics suggested that farmers preferred their pool of labourers to be desperate, but it would be fairer to say that they were nervous about providing rural labourers with land. Farming has always required urgent access to cheap labour at harvest time, and there were fears that allotments and smallholdings would make it more difficult for farmers to harvest their crops.

His first success came early. This was the Allotments Extension Act 1882, which said that land held for the poor must be let as allotments "to cottagers and labourers". This was a shot across the bows of those poor law commissioners or charity trustees that were sitting on parcels of land which could be put to use (it was finally repealed by the Major government in 1993). It was an

---

[7] Collings and Green (1920), 124.

important first step and it required some policing, so Collings set up the Allotments Extension Association to pressurise recalcitrant local trustees. It grew rapidly to publish its own newspaper, *Land and People.*

It was increasingly clear that the zeitgeist was on Collings' side. The land issue was rising up the political agenda and was at the very forefront of political debate. This was partly because of the well-publicised misery of farm labourers in Ireland, and the forced evictions which the Westminster government was determined to curtail, by giving rights to the land to Irish tenants. But it was also because of Chamberlain's increasingly radical energies, which had now burst onto the national stage. Chamberlain identified the narrow ownership of land in Britain as his major complaint against the privileges of the aristocracy. He and Collings campaigned closely together – Chamberlain in the cities, and Collings in the rural areas – and putting the land to wider use was a major theme.

When the grand old Liberal, John Bright, threw his weight behind them, it was clear that real change was possible. "The time is near in my opinion," he said, "when the great land monopoly of this country will be assailed and when it will be broken into and broken up."[8]

---

[8] *Manchester Guardian* (1880), 25 Mar.

Chamberlain lit the touchpaper of the political fireworks with an attack on the Conservative leader Lord Salisbury, describing him as "the spokesman of a class – a class to which he himself belongs, *who toil not neither do they spin*".[9]

At the heart of the land battle was the question of giving two million agricultural labourers the vote, under the assumption that they would then force through radical land legislation. There were huge demonstrations after the House of Lords at first threw out the extended franchise in 1884, with farm labourers marching into London from Kent and Sussex in a pattern faintly reminiscent of the Peasants Revolt. The *Daily News* spoke patronisingly of "men who carried fresh-cut walking sticks and who do not show the remotest affectation of the ways of town life".[10]

It was during the forthcoming general election in 1885 that Collings first used his famous slogan 'Three acres and a cow'. He tested it in a speech in Cirencester, and it was much ridiculed by his Conservative opponents, but it caught the spirit of the times, setting out clearly what he considered was the minimum for a family to live on.

---

[9] Joseph Chamberlain (1883), 30 Mar.
[10] Quoted in Collings and Green (1920), 171.

Chamberlain adopted the slogan for his Radical Programme, which set out how the state would buy land and let it to anyone who wanted it, at the rate of one acre of arable and four acres of pasture. This was the moment that the Liberal Party adopted some of the flavour of Ruskinian radicalism. "The standard of welfare of the large family we call the nation should be not so much the amount of its aggregate money wealth," wrote Collings, "but the moral, material and social condition of the great mass of its members."[11]

By 1886, the campaign was at its height. In retrospect, it was an extraordinary promise. How could an urban, industrial population get their three acres, let alone their cows – even just for those that wanted them? Yet something was happening. The 1882 act had produced 394,517 smallholdings of under four acres and 272,000 'garden allotments'. The early allotments raised awareness of the threat to other commons land, and campaigns spread locally. With their radical slogan, Chamberlain and Collings managed to link those concerns to the continuing sore of urban and rural poverty.

---

[11] Collings and Green (1920), 181.

Historians sometimes argue that the Unauthorised Programme had little impact.[12] But the allotments element was a political theme which echoed through the next six decades. Land access was the solution – not taxing land, the great campaign of the 1890s, because that simply accepted ownership patterns as they stood. Land was to be re-organised in such a way that anyone who wanted to access to it should be able to have it, whoever they were, wherever they lived.

Then in January 1886, Collings was suddenly centre stage. Rather to his own surprise, his amendment to the Queen's Speech, regretting that Lord Salisbury's Conservatives had no plans to help agricultural labourers find allotments and smallholdings, was passed by the House of Commons. It brought down the government, and became known as the 'Three Acres and a Cow' amendment.

At long last, the Liberal leader William Ewart Gladstone rose in his seat to support Collings during the debate, promising to "restore the old local communities of this country something of that character of a community, in which the common interests of the individual labourer

---

[12] See Ian Packer (2001), *Lloyd George, Liberalism and the Land: The land issue and party politics in England 1906-1914*, Royal Historical Society/Boydell Press, Woodbridge, 12-13.

may be so managed as to associate him with the soil in a manner much more effectively than that by which he is associated with it at present".[13]

Joseph Arch, also now just elected as Liberal MP for North West Norfolk, gave his maiden speech in support. A few days later, Gladstone took office at the head of a new Liberal government. Collings had never been so hopeful, but things were not quite as they seemed.

The first sign of trouble came when he introduced his Allotments and Small Holdings Bill, designed to give parishes the power to provide allotments where there was a demand and nowhere was available at a reasonable rent. To his consternation, the new government failed to adopt it. Instead, Gladstone pushed forward his deeply controversial Irish Home Rule Bill, determined once and for all to end the centuries of dispute with Ireland. It was a brave move, but Collings and his colleagues were enraged that so much urgent radical legislation was being postponed for a Home Rule measure they hardly found convincing.

Chamberlain was particularly angry and felt himself overlooked. He resigned from the government in March, forming an uneasy alliance of Liberal radicals and Liberal

---

[13] Collings and Green (1920), 185-6.

conservatives who, for various different reasons, opposed Irish Home Rule. The Liberal Unionists, as they came to be called, were numerous enough to form a government with Lord Salisbury, though Chamberlain and his radical allies stayed on the outside for the time being. Frenetic negotiations to reunite the Liberal Party broke down, but Chamberlain began negotiating aspects of his radical programme with Salisbury. By 1888, the rift was no longer repairable, but it suddenly seemed possible that the alliance between Conservatives and Liberal Unionists might deliver many aspects of Collings' dreams.

It was a traumatic period of betrayal and shattered friendships. Arch stayed with the Gladstonian Liberals while Collings and the land reformers followed Chamberlain. Collings was flung out of his own Allotments Extension Association, which was then in the hands of the Gladstonians. Instead, he set up the new Rural Labourers League, with Chamberlain in the chair, which became a formidable campaign organisation in its own right, with 25 paid local agents and 3,000 volunteers nationwide.

Despite this stressful and upsetting process, Collings went on campaigning, battling for his bill through increasingly elongated sessions until he could do no more. The issues were put to the test in a by-election in

Spalding in Lincolnshire, which was unexpectedly won by a Liberal on the allotments issue. By then, he had decided to save what he could, and split his bill into two. What was passed was the Allotments and Cottage Gardens Compensation for Crops Act 1887, which obliged local authorities to provide allotments if there was a demand for them. Allotments later became the key issue in the first county council elections in 1889. Even the evolution pioneer Alfred Russel Wallace joined in the campaign by applying for an allotment to the new Dorset County Council and then publicising the delays and barriers thrown in his way by reluctant officials. Even so, three years later, another 150,000 people had allotments.

In March 1891, Collings finally passed the other half, his Smallholdings Bill. It had taken him eleven years of constant campaigning, reintroducing the bill with every session, rather as Sir John Lubbock had done with his Ancient Monuments Act. "I have in the last five years seen more progress made with the practical application of my political programme than in all my previous life," wrote Chamberlain shortly afterwards. "I owe this result entirely to my former opponents, and all the opposition has come from my former friends."

But here the new political divisions began to make themselves felt. Collings passionately believed that the smallholdings should be owned outright, as similar legislation allowed for in Ireland. He wanted his new peasant class to be proprietors, not dependent on landlords, even if those landlords were the county councils. He drafted his Purchase of Land Bill in 1895, designed to let ordinary farm tenants buy their farms, by advancing them the money to do so, and doing the same for people who wanted to be smallholders. He reintroduced it every year until 1914. It never made it into law.

The problem was that the politics of the debate was changing. Gladstone's final administration gave powers to parish councils to acquire allotments, but they were to be rented, not sold or given away. The land tax debate was now emerging and Collings' former colleagues in the Liberals were less interested in providing new forms of land ownership, and increasingly interested in using the tax system to take away the power of the landowners – not adding to their number.

Collings' influence on Chamberlain's son Austen was bringing Conservatives round to the idea of a new class of owners on the land – as long as the smallholdings were not so big that labourers became independent of farmers.[14] The Conservative Lord Onslow launched his Association for the Voluntary Extension of the Allotments System as a way to head off their fears that the Liberals would nationalise the land.

At the same time, Collings' smallholdings campaign was attracting the determined opposition of the new Labour Party. Ramsay Macdonald himself opposed him in a ten minute rule bill debate in 1907. The idea of land ownership, even by the poorest, was anathema to socialists. Collings' other political problem was that his Liberal Unionists now barely existed. Chamberlain had become a ferocious imperialist, and Colonial Secretary in the government, and the Liberal Unionist party organisation was to be wound up completely in 1912.

Worse, the Liberal landslide at the beginning of 1906 anyway swept the Unionists from power. Chamberlain took the opportunity to swoop on a weakened Conservative Party and to effectively seize the leadership for his radical imperialism. But just as his moment of triumph, he was struck down by a paralysing stroke. His wife Mary found his dressing room locked from the inside and, terrified, sent for a crowbar. Before it arrived,

---

[14] See Paul Readman (2008) *Land and Nation in England: Patriotism, national identity and the politics of land 1880-1914*, Royal Historical Society/Boydell Press, Woodbridge, 20.

the door was unlocked and Chamberlain crawled out. He did not return to the House of Commons for four years, and then only briefly after the 1910 election to be sworn in, his right foot dragging behind him and his speech slow and hard to recognise.

The radical Liberal David Lloyd George maintained the old Collings line as late as 1910. "I hope Liberalism will see its way to go even further than ensuring security of tenure for those who cultivate the soil," he told the audience at the Queen's Hall in London.[15] "Our chairman has already indicated that in his judgement there should be some great measure which would transfer the ownership of the soil from the great landowners to the cultivating peasants."

But the politics was different now. The main thrust of the new Liberal government was to build on the idea of security of tenure and they saw it differently to Collings. "The magic of property, such as it is, is derived not from ownership but from security," said H. H. Asquith, the Home Secretary.[16]

So when the Liberals' twin Smallholdings and Allotments Bills emerged, in 1907 and 1908, security not

---

[15] J. Collings (1914), *The Colonization of Rural Britain, Rural World, London,* Vol 2, 332-3.
[16] Collings and Green (1920), 273.

ownership was the objective. In fact, would-be smallholders had to find a fifth of the purchase money themselves. This was the proposal of a commission chaired by the banker Sir Edward Holden, who said that a new land bank should only advance four fifths of the price at 4 per cent interest. Worse, new smallholding tenants would have to pay the interest on the loan to buy the land for their farms, but the ownership would still stay with the county councils. "It is, in short a communalization of the land, not at the expense of the hated landlord, but at that of the 'sweated' tenant," said a furious Collings.[17]

The smallholdings aspect of the new law was a failure: less than 5,000 new smallholders took the plunge, mainly in market gardens near the big cities, but it was different for allotments. The 1907 Act was consolidated into the 1908 Act, and gives local authorities more duties to provide allotments to people who want them (there was a furore in 2011 when the government indicated they were going to repeal it). But Jesse Collings, the great advocate of allotments – the key figure in their history in the UK – voted against it. His remaining allies tried to extend the rights of tenant farmers to buy their farms with

---

[17] Collings (1914), 339.

state help when they were for sale, but their amendment was lost by 56 votes.

By the end of the decade, even Lloyd George was on the other side. "Great Britain, in my judgement, is utterly unsuited to the establishment of a great peasant proprietorship," he said.[18]   It was a bitter blow to Collings, who was now in ill-health and desperate to give up his parliamentary seat.   The great cause he had given his political career to seemed to have finally been defeated.   What he had actually achieved, embedding allotments into the new local government machine, was vital for the future, but it was so little compared to the scale of his ambition: to get people back on the land, even in the cities.

Lloyd George launched his own land campaign in 1913, borrowing Collings' radical language about the rural English, but to argue for land tax, conjuring up a vision of the sturdy, traditional peasant:

"He had his common (cheers) where he could graze a cow that would give him milk and butter for himself and his children. There was a little patch where he could raise corn to feed them. There he had his poultry, his geese, his

---

[18] This was in July 1913, see Collings (1914), 333.

pigs; a patch of land where he could raise green produce for the table. He was a gentlemen; he was independent. He had a stake in his country. His title was as ancient and apparently as indefensible as that of the lord of the manor. Where had it gone to? Stolen."[19]

It was radical. It may have resulted in major extensions to land available for allotments if the First World War had not intervened, but it wasn't what Collings had campaigned for. In March 1909, a disappointed Collings slipped on the icy footboard of a train at Charing Cross Station, fell on the platform and fractured his hip. He never entirely recovered, but he was paradoxically to see a peculiar and extremely sudden revival of his political fortunes.

---

[19] *The Times* (1913), Oct 12.

V

"Not until a year ago were allotment gardens officially regarded as a factor of importance in the sense that they contributed substantially to the home-grown food supplies of this country."
Gerald Butcher, *Allotments for All*, 1918

The month of November 1916, the mid-point of the First World War, was a worrying one for the embattled allies. The British field commander, Sir Douglas Haig, finally called a halt to the Battle of the Somme which, since the previous July, had seen 95,000 British and empire dead. The Russian government collapsed and British ministers were beginning to doubt whether Asquith – now leading a war coalition government – had his mind wholly on the job. There were some members of the government who were looking ahead to the following year with serious trepidation.

One of these was the Earl of Crawford, a former Conservative chief whip, and later to be a leading figure in the development of the National Trust and the Victoria and Albert Museum. Crawford was also eclectic enough to have been a friend of William Morris. He had recently been working as a liaison officer on the Western front with the French press and was surprised to be asked by his party leader if he would like to become President of the Board of Agriculture.

He only occupied the position briefly, but what he found in his first days in Whitehall terrified him. The tonnage of British shipping sunk by U-boats in the Atlantic was mounting and was reaching crisis proportions, losing anything up to 10,000 tons a day. The new head of the navy, Sir John Jellicoe, appointed in November was already engaged in the bitter disagreements about whether to introduce the same convoy system that had been used so successfully in the Napoleonic Wars. By the spring or early summer, before the next harvest, Crawford could see perfectly clearly – just as his officials could – there was a serious danger that the nation would run out of food.

Crawford organised a series of meetings with senior ministers through the bloody late summer of 1916, urging them to see the reality – that Britain was besieged and needed to act accordingly. Asquith worried him by looking to what he called "generous providence".

The first few months of 1917 were to prove Crawford right. Shipping losses rose to over 600,000 tons a month, which was the figure the German High Command believed would starve Britain into submission within six months. Wheat supplies dropped to just six weeks worth. In the ice and drizzle, there was panic buying of potatoes – the absolutely staple food – and nervous memories of the Irish Potato Famine only seven decades before. People were queuing for hours, sometimes up to their ankles in frozen water, to get enough to feed their families. There was an eruption of public anger.

The beginning of the war had seen moves by the government to promote allotments, and to urge people to grow more food in their back gardens. King George V made sure that vegetables were growing in the flowerbeds of Windsor Castle and Buckingham Palace, and in front of the palace too. But this was mainly political rhetoric and, at the end of 1916, Crawford believed something else was needed.

He did have one important ally, at least in promoting the communalisation of food production. This was the Vacant Land Cultivation Society, a new pressure group set up in 1907 by the American soap millionaire Joseph Fels, following a series of controversial land invasions on the outskirts of cities by people who wanted to grow food. Fels had been at the forefront of the vacant lot societies that had emerged at the end of the nineteenth century in so many American cities, as a way of linking "idle land with idle labour".

But his 'farm colonies' in Essex ran into trouble immediately. The future father of the welfare state, William Beveridge, then assistant to the social reformer Canon Samuel Barnett, studied them and dismissed them as just a form of casual labour for unemployed people. Fels had more success in Dublin, where the Jesuit priest Joseph McDonnell had made huge progress buying up small plots of land and letting them to casual labourers.

By November 1916, Crawford was not aware that, behind the scenes, a coup was in the process of being organised. Lloyd George was about to take over the coalition government, which would leave both Asquith and Crawford out of office. But by then, the key policy shift had been made. Crawford called in the Vacant Land Cultivation Society to ask their advice about what he was planning. Included in the meeting was the Society's enthusiastic organising director for London, Gerald Butcher.

Butcher explained that after "an interview lasting an hour or more, [we] left with the full knowledge that probably the greatest drama which had taken place in land reform for many generations was about to be enacted..."

"For once, at any rate, the privilege of the few was to become the right of the many. By virtue of the powers conferred by the Defence of the Realm Regulations, the government was about to lay its hand upon the most sacred of monopolies, the most jealously guarded of all vested interests; it intended, briefly, to commandeer certain land in order that allotments might be provided on a large and unprecedented scale."[20]

Two weeks later, Crawford made his plans public. The result was the Cultivation of Lands Order 1916. It gave county councils the right to take over waste land or abandoned land, without the consent or even knowledge of its owners, and use it to grow food. Crawford had been nervous that the order would outrage people, but in fact the local authorities were overwhelmed with demand from people applying to turn specific bits of land into allotments, or to take over part of the new allotments themselves.

Where the measure was controversial was in London. The officials at the London County Council (LCC), as it was then, were dead set against the idea. There were angry demonstrations around the Furzedown Estate in

---

[20] Gerald W. Butcher (1918) *Allotments for All: The story of a great movement*, George Allen & Unwin, London, 18.

Tooting where there had been hundreds of applications for allotments on waste ground that owners would not lend out. Half the land was eventually handed over just before Christmas.

But Furzedown and two acres at Plumstead were as far as the LCC would go – and they took back the Plumstead land shortly afterwards to use for football pitches. The result was a powerful campaign led by the *London Evening News* which persuaded some of the London boroughs to go it alone. Wandsworth went direct to the Board of Agriculture and got permission to take over the land which the LCC had denied them. There was soon an avalanche of other applications as the boroughs were overwhelmed with applicants, just as local authorities were elsewhere in the nation. It was a phenomenon that the press called 'allotmentitis', which described the addiction that ordinary men and women – and the women also caused comment – had to working out in the open growing food.

Allotmentitis spread quickly. Lloyd George let it be known that he was growing potatoes at home. The Archbishop of Canterbury issued a special letter allowing people to work on allotments on Sundays. Dig for Victory is famous from the Second World War, and has largely blotted out memory of related revolution that happened far faster during the First World War – really in just two years, from 1917 to 1918 – and which was far more focused on the idea of allotments than the better organised campaign that began in 1939.

Cobbett's insight from a century before, that poor land could be made productive with close attention, also became apparent again. One allotment holder wrote to Butcher:

"Owing to the apparently practical impossibility of ever making anything of this plot, I believe two previous holders threw it up as quite unworkable, and when I took it over, which was not until last Easter, I found it to consist of an absolute swamp at the end next the road. About a quarter of its full extent was completely covered with water, varying in depth from three inches to over a foot, whilst the greater part of the remainder was covered with accumulations of builders' rubbish, some of the heaps being over five feet high. I often had nasty remarks thrown at my head as to whether I intended to grow watercress, go in for trout fishing, or let out pleasure-boats on my allotment, so you can perhaps judge what a terrible fight I have had to make it a practical garden. However, I think I may be excused for saying I feel quite proud of the fact that, in spite of what I have been repeatedly told was an impossibility, by dint of sheer hard work I have conquered its drawbacks. I have trenched all my ground to a depth of 3 to 3½ feet, and have been rewarded by a splendid crop of turnips, a good supply of potatoes, and fairly decent crops of other vegetables. I may also mention I have grown some good sugar beet, and some of my roots have been sent out to a soldier in France who has a craving for some but wrote that there was none to be obtained in that country. I have a very promising supply of green crops on the land for the winter and spring, and am looking forward to being able to work my allotment next season without such heart-breaking trials and hard labour as I have been through this season."[21]

Cobbett's other discovery, that small-scale agriculture can be more productive than large scale agriculture, was also clear again – at least to *Country Life* magazine:

"The assumption on which a national policy of agriculture is based seems to be that the food supply of the country depends chiefly on the large cultivators. One is not prepared to say that there is no truth in this. The

---

[21] Butcher (1918), 29

five-hundred acre farm must yield a greater absolute percentage of the food supply than the little plots. Still, that is not all the truth... Some remarkable instances can be given to show how this works out practically. For example, a man who had cultivated forty rods of land, when he set about it was able to produce as much from twenty rods as he had done from forty rods."[22]

But what really excited Butcher and his supporters in the National Allotments Society (as it became known) was the dropping price of potatoes, after the crisis during the winter. By the end of June 1917, the government ordered hotels not to serve them, except on Tuesdays and Fridays. But the allotment potato harvest was beginning to come in and the price was dropping. "This was undoubtedly the greatest triumph allotment-holders have ever achieved — for it was their achievement," wrote Butcher.[23] Now that imported food like tea and meat began to be really scarce, vegetables were now in good supply, only eight months since Crawford's order.

As a result, some churches held services of thanksgiving on Rogation Sunday, and held them out of doors, processing around the church with the plotholders

[22] *Country Life* (1917) 29 Sept.
[23] Butcher (1918), 68.

and their families following the choir, and bearing their digging tools.

The allotments of the First World War were a social phenomenon and their effects were to echo through society long after the plots had been handed back to the housing developers. Many of those using them for growing vegetables had no idea how to distribute their produce, and refused to sell it – but gave it away around the neighbourhood as a sign of largesse. Those who did sell it found, on average that allotment growing could produce food to the value of £80 an acre – in the days when a hefty bag of potatoes cost 5d (about 2p).[24] The argument for allotments as a tool of poverty reduction seemed to have been won.

People like Gerald Butcher also promoted the new allotments as engines of social change, as venues for adult education and lectures, and as levers of co-operation. The days when they were the preserve of people in poverty, or even outdoor people miserably transplanted to urban areas, seemed to have gone for good. Everybody could be involved.

There was even a crack in the old idea that allotments were the preserve of men. It was only a crack. Women at

---

[24] Butcher (1918), 31.

work on their plots sometimes drew small crowds to cheer them on, rather patronisingly, or nod their heads knowingly when the job got too heavy. But so many men were away fighting, so of course the idea of 'Dad's plot' was no longer sustainable. The Back to the Land movement had clung to traditional gender roles, and would go on doing so for another generation, but the end was in sight.

In some ways, Lloyd George's coalition saw a last gasp of Liberal Unionism. This was a combination of Conservatism and Liberal radicalism, especially in its battle with poverty, with an added extra dimension of the Lloyd George's energetic way of doing things, breaking with tradition and accepted wisdom in the hurry to get things done. This was especially so when it came to the problem of returning soldiers from the huge army on the Western Front.

The introduction of the Land Settlement (Facilities) Bill of December 1918, designed to resettle returning soldiers on the land, provided a welcome glimmer of hope for Collings that all was not lost. Collings was ill (he died in 1920) but his friends organised a successful amendment allowing smallholders to buy their land after six years, and to pay back the money over 60 years. By the time he died, another 208,000 acres had been acquired for former soldiers and Collings died believing that his campaign was back on track.

It wasn't of course. County council smallholdings have been amalgamated since and slowly sold. The early 1920s also saw a very rapid unravelling of the allotments movement, and the number of allotments fell back below a million in 1929. It was the speculative building boom which swallowed up all those new, energetic allotment sites on marginal land on the edge of the cities. Soon they were giving way to the 'ribbon development' that so horrified critics like the architect Clough Williams-Ellis.[25] But paradoxically, even the building boom was laying the foundations of a whole new kind of urban agriculture.

The new suburbs, providing the 'homes fit for heroes' promised by Lloyd George, around the cities, offered low-cost home ownership in semi-detached houses, designed without the aid of architects and packed with the symbolism of country living – the gabled front doors, the winding front garden paths and garden gates. They were within the reach of anyone on a salary, with mortgages costing ten per cent of their income for fifteen years.

But most important, they were homes with gardens. There was a patch of green at the back for cultivation, or

---

[25] Clough Williams-Ellis (ed.) (1938) *Britain and the Beast*, J. M. Dent, London.

for hens or even the occasional pig. They were laid out with extraordinary generosity, compared to modern housing estates, at twelve to an acre – and powerfully influenced by the garden cities of Letchworth and Welwyn, where Ebenezer Howard had planned homes with plots that were a hundred feet deep. These were not smallholdings; they weren't even allotments, but this was the way in which the access to land envisaged by Collings came to shift the way we live.

Despite Williams-Ellis, the suburban semi was in some ways the most successful home design in British history. They were successful partly because of the rural symbolism, and partly because of the green space. But they also echoed another national obsession: the rising panic around the First World War about the state of the nation's health, and a clamour to tackle the 'physical degeneration' of the Anglo-Saxon race. It wasn't just about producing food, said the novelist Rider Haggard, it was about preserving the British character.[26]

This was a new note, strident and nationalistic, which had been absent from the Back to the Land movement before. It would soon take the movement, and the advocates of allotments, to some disturbing places.

---

[26] H. Haggard (1902) *Rural England*, Longmans, London.

But despite the failure of the First World War allotments movement to develop, there was a sign that some of the more modern concerns with allotments were being articulated – the impact on health and the vital importance of contact with the land. But even Gerald Butcher, writing in 1918, saw this in patriotic terms:

"There is a sympathetic connection, an inherent kinship between man and the land; a link which generations of landless people have failed to break. In the veins of every Englishman runs the blood of the old-time yeoman of the soil, who lived an active life on and by the land in years of peace, and in times of national stress formed the bulwark of the Empire.... And that is why, having again come into contact with the land, this great mass of patriotic citizens means to stick to it, or turn out governments in the attempt."[27]

Sadly, they were not able to 'stick to it', but an opportunity would come again, all too soon.

---

[27] Butcher (1918), 64-5.

VI

"Tinned meat, tinned fish, tinned milk, tinned beans, tinned minds, tinned breath…"

John Betjeman, 'Come friendly bombs and fall on Slough', 1937

Sir Reginald Dorman-Smith was governor of Burma in 1941 when the Japanese marched in. He had been one of the youngest ever presidents of the National Farmers Union, and he was also was Neville Chamberlain's agriculture minister at the outbreak of war. It was Dorman-Smith who made the famous broadcast in October 1939 which launched the 'Dig for Victory' campaign, a deliberate attempt to revive the 'allotmentitis' of the First World War. It was one of the most memorable slogans of the whole conflict, an extraordinary extension of the allotments idea, and some indication of how Gerald Butcher and his allies would have developed if their own allotment movement had lasted six years instead of two.

But Dorman-Smith was not as conventional as he seemed. He was born in Ireland. One brother was a captain in the Royal Navy and another brother was a general in the British army, before resigning to devote himself to Irish nationalism. But it is the strange network of Reginald Dorman-Smith's friends that is especially relevant here. He was a member in the 1930s of an ultra-conservative ginger group, called English Mistery, founded by a disaffected Freemason and diehard monarchist called William Sanderson. English Mistery envisaged an England, not just for the English but divided along feudal lines, with country rituals and the nation digging like mad. The Back to the Land movement had been associated with the far left in the 1880s. By the 1930s, it was becoming associated instead with the far right.

How could allotments and access to the land be radically left wing one moment and radically right wing idea only decades later? Partly it was Collings' influence in the Conservative Party. Partly it was the growing panic about a 'stunted race', trapped in the cities. But the reason the allotments ideal began to revive as a right-wing solution is largely down to two revolutionary campaigners, neither of whom were conventionally conservative and neither of whom were paradoxically very interested in allotments.

The first of these was Hilaire Belloc, mainly known these days for his *Cautionary Tales*, but in his day a strident mixture of historian, economic campaigner and Roman Catholic apologist. It was left to Belloc and his great friend G. K. Chesterton, both former Liberals (Belloc was MP for Salford South), to revive Collings' campaign and slogan and to add a new layer of complexity to the Back to the Land tradition. Belloc's book *The Servile State* (1912) was an influential diatribe against both big business and Fabian collectivist policies - now rather inappropriately kept in print by obscure American libertarians, which wouldn't have pleased him. The book formed the basis of the political movement known as Distributism that flourished in the 1920s.

Distributism knitted together the old Catholic social doctrine of Pope Leo XIII and Cardinal Manning, that was so close to Belloc's heart. It developed Collings' idea that owning a small plot of land underpinned human liberty. It also kept alive the 'three acres and a cow' slogan. In fact, because of Belloc, the slogan continued to be associated with the Liberal Party well into the second half of the twentieth century, but with little understanding about its origins or objectives.

Distributism was anti-industrial, anti-finance, anti-corporation, anti-bureaucrat, and most of all anti-giantism, either big bureaucracy or big business – the 'Big Rot' according to Belloc. What it was actually for was a little hazier, but it included Jeffersonian solutions of workers' co-operatives, smallholdings and savings boosted by the state – and giving people access to the land. One of their earliest campaigns was in support of the small London bus companies that were being driven out by the monopolistic London General Omnibus Company. In response, they bought a series of Distributist buses, painted them red, green and blue and called them things like 'William Morris' - and took on the big company buses.[28]

The Distributist campaign fizzled out after the Second World War. Those who took it most to heart were not the urban poor, but craftsmen like Eric Gill or journalists like Beachcomber. Part of the problem was that it failed to develop a practical programme. Chesterton's scintillating book *Outline of Sanity* is couched in terms of a last ditch stand against the inevitable.[29] It is deeply melancholic, the besetting sin of the Back to the Land movement in all ages.

Belloc's politics were by then drifting in unpredictable directions. He flirted with French monarchism, with Mussolini and Franco. His views about Europe's Jewish heritage were complicated enough

[28] A. N. Wilson (1984) *Hilaire Belloc*, Hamish Hamilton, London.
[29] G. K. Chesterton (1926) *Outline of Sanity*, Methuen, London.

for him to be accused of anti-semitism – and like T. S. Eliot, his reputation has been tarred with that ever since – though he recognised Hitler for what he was from the start and warned about his threat to the Jews. Chesterton's *GK's Weekly* pedalled a fashionable anti-semitic edge.

The Catholic Land League tried to put some measure of Distributism into action, providing plots for the unemployed during the Depression, but they ran into difficulties, as always, with unemployment benefit regulations.

The Quakers were a little more successful, aware that people were abandoning allotments when they needed them most because they could no longer afford seeds. They persuaded the Ministry of Labour to rule that income from selling vegetables from allotments would not be means-tested. They even began supplying seeds and tools to unemployed people. This scheme was so successful that it was taken over by the government, and it helped 64,000 people through the winter of 1930. The embattled National Government cut the scheme the following year and the Quakers began all over again. It had a strange history: becoming the Land Settlement Association, then nationalised after the war, privatised again by Margaret Thatcher in 1984 when it became

Homegrown Salads. It is now part of the Icelandic firm Bakkavör.[30]

Belloc's Distributism was in some ways the precise opposite of the Fascism that was emerging across Europe, but it was similarly romantic in its interpretation of the world. In the new decade, romantic politics seemed to be largely right-wing. What is more, there has always been a tendency among those who believe there is a conspiracy of bankers – and the Back to the Land tradition has always maintained that – to believe it is also a conspiracy of *Jewish* bankers. The 1930s was hardly a moment that anyone was going to love the banks, but this was a dangerous time to start pedalling conspiracy theories.

The second pivotal figure in the shift in the 1930s was a charismatic and largely forgotten maverick called John Hargrave, or – as he called himself – White Fox. In the year that Collings died, Hargrave resigned as the Boy Scout movement's commissioner for camping after a rift with Robert Baden-Powell. He launched instead an extraordinary organisation known as Kibbo Kift, complete with new rituals, striking designs and an outdoor life, inspired by the romantic German *wandervogel* tradition.

---

[30] *The Land* (2011), Winter.

Kibbo Kift eventually split. The socialist wing broke away to form the Woodcraft Folk, still going strong today, but Hargrave became convinced that the banking system was threatening world peace and transformed his campers overnight into a militaristic political party dedicated to an economic policy of social credit, the idea that governments not banks should create money to provide a basic income to everyone as of right The Greenshirts, as they were known, dressed in uniforms inspired by Mussolini's and had running street battles with Mosley's Blackshirts (though Mosley was also committed to social credit).

Hargrave provided a conduit by which German outdoor romanticism fed into British culture, at a time when unpleasant things were happening in Germany. He was not one of those who believed that the outdoor life should involve growing things, but his 'gleemaster' in Kibbo Kift, Rolf Gardiner, thought otherwise.

Gardiner took over his uncle's farm in Dorset to host summer youth camps, folk music and dancing , with a mystical sense of the English countryside. He was a friend and disciple of D. H. Lawrence and shared some of his sense of the mystery and magic of the soil. He remains a controversial figure. Gardiner was part Jewish himself, though he flirted with far right groups between the wars, and his reputation suffered from his perfectly civilised habit of greeting German prisoners-of-war – who had come to work on his Springhead estate – in their native tongue.

But his main importance here is as a key figure in the development of organic farming, and one of the founders of the Soil Association. His mystical anti-urban views, and the idea that a return to small-scale agriculture was vital to underpin the future of the nation, were widely shared among a broad group of writers, including H. J. Massingham and Jorian Jenks, later agricultural advisor to the British Union of Fascists – and Reginald Dorman-Smith, the man who launched Dig for Victory. Most of them joined Dorman-Smith in English Mistery before the fatal split which led to Viscount Lymington's more proto-fascist, more avowedly anti-semitic English Array. Jenks went on to edit the Soil Association's magazine after the war.

Like Belloc, these were ultra-conservatives, monarchists and feudalists with a dislike of Americans and bankers, sceptical of big industrial agriculture and corporate power. Unlike Belloc or Hargrave, they talked about reviving 'English stock', defending the race, and the crucial importance of drinking unpasteurised milk. They shared a particular horror of processed or tinned food, which they believed was corroding the nation's health.

Back to the Land was promoted as part of Oswald Mosley's British Union of Fascists (BUF) platform. His enthusiastic acolyte, the novelist Henry Williamson, took it so seriously that he bought a farm in Norfolk and struggled with farming it throughout the war. Jenks' agricultural policies, which attracted Williamson to join the BUF, envisaged a kind of fortress Britain, growing all its own food – plus fixed prices, low-rate loans for farmers, small scale farming and a massive extension of allotments.

Hitler, Mussolini and Mosley were all modernists. They were not interested in the sheer individualism of small farmers and allotment growers. The plot of land as a guarantee of freedom would have been enough to make them as suspicious as Stalin was of the *kulaks*, and for the same reason. But there is no doubt that – for some time – they attracted the leading lights in their generation of Back to the Land enthusiasts, because the far right was the focus for opposition to issues they felt strongly about, corporate power, the arrogance of banks and the degradation of the soil. These were the years, not just of the Great Depression, but also of the American dust bowl.

There is now doubt also, when Dorman-Smith launched his Dig for Victory campaign, backed by many of these same policies, that he was deeply influenced by the romantic ideas of English Mistery as well as the practical necessities of wartime: the sturdy peasantry of England, wielding their forks in defiance. This is what he said in the historic Dig for Victory broadcast:

"In normal times our own farms produce nearly half our food requirements … While of course we can rely on our Navy to keep our trade routes open, and while we will still be able to draw on food supplies from our Dominions and other countries, those supplies may not always be unlimited. It is clearly our duty, just as it is a matter of elementary wisdom, to try to make doubly and trebly sure that we will fight and win this war on full stomachs. To do this we want not only the big man with the plough, but the little man with the spade to get busy this autumn. … Half a million allotments properly worked will provide potatoes and vegetables that will feed another million adults and one and a half million children for eight months out of twelve. The matter is not one that can wait. So – let's get going. Let 'Dig for Victory' be the motto of every able-bodied man and women capable of digging an allotment in their spare time."[31]

Dig for Victory remains one of the most successful attempts to galvanise the public, transforming their gardens into mini-allotments, digging up parks and other corners of public land to make more. From 815,000 allotments in 1939 the number rose to 1.4 million by 1943, by which time over a million tons of vegetables a year were being grown in gardens and allotments. There were radio programmes (3.5 million people tuned into C. H. Middleton's gardening slots), information leaflets, even Dig for Victory anthems. There were propaganda films about people queuing for food – "it's not the greengrocers fault, it's up to you" – showing vegetables emerging from roofs, the tops of air raid shelters or the old playgrounds of bombed out schools.

It was an extraordinary endeavour and there were official attempts to keep the campaign going under the slogan 'Dig for Plenty', but somehow the Never-Had-It-So-Good years seemed to let the allotment movement drift away. There were still 1.4m plots by 1950, but by

---

[31] BBC (1939), 3 Oct.

1960 there were only 800,000 (12.6% vacant) and by 1970 there were only 530,000 (20% vacant).[32]

Something had changed. Perhaps it was the end of rationing in (1954), and the beginning of self-service supermarkets (1950) which ushered in a different sense of plenty. Perhaps remains of the old sturdy working class image of allotments made them seem old-fashioned. Perhaps also the romanticism of the allotments movement was considered dangerous in a technocratic age.

This might explain the sense of official neglect that followed the end of Dig for Victory and Dig for Plenty. Those who had advocated self-help agriculture before the Second World War had certainly been romantics, but some of them had been interned during the war as dangerous enemies of the state – including Jorian Jenks. There has been a collective terror of romanticism in politics among the Westminster elite ever since. The Westminster and Whitehall elite prefer cool-headed technocracy. What could they do about the Back to the land movement, or Gerald Butcher's "yearning for the soil"? They had a housing crisis on their hands, and then a balance of payments crisis and then an energy crisis – and all the other crises that have beset the British

---

[32] David Crouch and Colin Ward (1988) *The Allotment: Its landscape and culture,* Faber & Faber, London, 77.

establishment since the war. Their attention turned
elsewhere.

VII

"Oh! It really is a very pretty garden,
And Chingford to the eastward could be seen;
Wiv a ladder and some glasses,
You could see to 'Ackney Marshes,
If it wasn't for the 'ouses in between."
Edgar Bateman, 'If it wasn't for the 'ouses in between', 1894

The Balham musical hall singer Gus Elen began as a busker in the 1880s, when Collings was starting his land campaign, and made his way to the top by pretending to be a dreamy costermonger, trapped in a terraced flat, dreaming of the country views he ought to have been able to see from his garden – "if it wasn't for the 'ouses in between'.

The rural dream is as English as steak and kidney pie, and Elen expressed it in a way that struck a chord with his audiences, and not just by making fun of his character. He was recognising that this was a dream shared by rich and poor alike, including those who are now trapped in the worst concrete environments in the inner cities. "The dust-cart, though it seldom comes, is just like 'arvest 'ome," Elen sang, coming on stage armed with watering can and a wilting pot plant. A third of UK city-dwellers would like to move out, so there is a bit of Gus Elen in many of us.[33]

Of course the song makes fun of the pretensions of the lower classes. It is a snobbish performance, but it isn't just that. That hopeless cry 'if it wasn't for the 'ouses in between' was echoed in the hearts of the audiences that heard it, just as it was echoed in Morris' utopian novel *News from Nowhere* two years later in 1896, where the narrator wakes up to find London has been replaced by a small-scale rural idyll. Morris' "dream of London small and white and clean/The clear Thames bordered by its gardens green" had come true.[34]

It was echoed in Ebenezer Howard's garden city campaign and in the mass marketing of low-cost homes with gardens in the middle years of the twentieth century. It was there in the first issues of *Ideal Home* and similar magazines in the 1920, with their features about hens and vegetables in the back garden, just as it is there for urban readers of *Country Living* today.

It has taken a century for this rural yearning for city-dwellers to be recognised. But now, as many as 92 per

---

[33] *Financial Times* (1992), 2 Nov.
[34] William Morris (2002) *The Earthly Paradise*, (Ed. Florence Boos), Routledge, London, 255.

cent feel it is important for them to have public gardens, parks, commons or other green spaces nearby.[35] There have been a series of studies showing that access to greenery can calm prisoners, help patients recover from operations more quickly and cut the risk of dementia (by up to 36 per cent).[36]

This is recognised in the academic literature, but barely acknowledged in public policy, and we have lived through two generations when it was recognised by neither. Quite the reverse. A new cadre of architects in local government believed that the kind of soil-based co-operation was unnecessary in the new world of concrete or high-rise redevelopment. Some city officials were gripped by a messianic fervour against informal, self-made landscapes. "We are dealing with people who have no initiative or civic pride," said Newcastle's chief planning officer in 1963, revealing the contempt of the governing classes for the governed. "The task surely is to break up such groupings, even though people seem to be

---

[35] Defra (2011) 2011 *Survey of public attitudes and behaviours towards the environment*, HMSO, London.
[36] Thrive (2009), *Dementia and Gardening*, Department of Health, London.

satisfied with their miserable environment and seem to enjoy an extrovert social life in their own locality."[37]

By the 1980s, this had settled down to a more cynical concern for 'efficiencies'. Municipal flower beds required maintenance so they were replaced with tarmac (a choice of red or green). If there was any nature allowed, then it was municipal grass with no sign of any vegetables. English planners have a weakness for grass "so that Christopher Robin can go hoppety-hop," said the great American planning critic Jane Jacobs.[38] They certainly have.

By then the allotments movement had passed its nadir, which we might taken to be 1969, when the government asked Professor Harry Thorpe from Birmingham University to advise them what to do. Thorpe was tireless in his efforts, finding that many allotments had been all but abandoned and looked like eyesores, reserved for that section of the working classes – retired policemen or railway porters – who were used to being out of doors. He made 44 recommendations, including the idea that allotments should replaced by the

---

[37] Quoted in Colin Ward (1989) *Welcome, Thinner City*, Bedford Square Press, London, 39.
[38] Jane Jacobs (1961) *The Death and Life of the Great American Cities*, Random House, New York, 109.

continental idea of 'leisure gardens', where growing things would no longer be the main function. None of the recommendations were accepted by the government. Something about allotments still made politicians shudder, as if they were the kind of caricature of working class life that looked worryingly old-fashioned to Labour and Conservative alike.

What was left was the very tail end of the Dig for Victory campaign, people who had got into the wartime allotment habit – people who had no connection with, and maybe little interest in, Cobbett, Collings or the Back to the Land movement. A quarter of a century on, that generation was dying out.

But even at the low point, something seemed to be stirring. The counterculture was beckoning. City Farm 1 in Kentish Town – re-using the scenery from the West End production of *No, No, Nanette* – had launched the city farms movement (1971). The chattering classes were buying *The Survival Handbook* – subtitled *'self-sufficiency for everyone'* – with detailed instructions about how to slaughter pigs (1975).[39] *The Good Life* was on television every week (1975 onwards). The first glimmerings of the artisan food movement were beginning to twinkle in the

---

[39] Michael Allaby et al (1975) *The Survival Handbook: Self-Sufficiency for Everyone*, Macmillan, London.

distance. Ten years after the Thorpe Report, Friends of the Earth was saying that the waiting lists for allotments were up by 1,600 per cent.[40]

What happened in the following decade has been an unprecedented peacetime rediscovery of the idea. The waiting lists crept up from 12,000 to well over 100,000 by 2008. There are now thought to be about six million people interested in having an allotment, with waiting lists as long as 40 years in one London borough.[41] Many councils have simply closed their waiting lists, so this may not be an accurate figure. The *Daily Telegraph*, no less, has described allotments as "both a sought after commodity and an essential social accessory".[42] Even the Queen turned a part of the garden in Buckingham Palace into a vegetable patch to provide for the palace kitchen. Seed companies have reported that, for the first time since the Second World War, they are selling more vegetable seeds than flower seeds.

What was it that created this huge shift? One argument suggests that it was an emerging scepticism

---

[40] Tara Garnett (1996) *Growing Food in Cities: A report to highlight and promote the benefits of urban agriculture in the UK*, National Food Alliance/SAFE Alliance, London.

[41] See Nick Hope and Victoria Ellis (2009) *Can You Dig It? Meeting community demand for allotments*, New Local Government Network, London, 13.

[42] Miller, A. (2008), 'Up the Allotments', *Daily Telegraph*, 24 May.

about mass food production, a suspicion about food additives, steroids in meat and chemicals on vegetables (it was this that brought so many young mothers into allotments). Another suggests was that it was the demand among immigrant cultures for vegetables that were simply not available commercially, or – especially among newly arrived Greeks or Portuguese families – that a small patch of land was a normal part of life (despite the Back to the Land politics of the 1930s, other cultures became a new backbone to the allotments idea). A third argument suggests that it was a demand for fresh veg, the idea that they should "taste of vegetables and not of supermarkets". Later, perhaps, it was a sense after the 2000 Petrol Blockade that the normal food distribution systems were far closer to collapse than anyone had realised before.

It is hard to pinpoint exactly what drove this huge change of heart, whether it was TV chefs campaigning for real food, the 'clone town' and Tescopoly campaigns focusing public anger at the monopolistic behaviour of supermarkets, or the Transition Towns movement negotiating more allotments locally as part of a shift to a low carbon economy. Whatever it was, it has been part of a wider shift in public attitudes which has also launched the local food movements in the West Country and has hitched the economic futures of places like Todmorden or Ludlow to their ability to deal in local food. It is also a reaction against the way houses have been built to higher densities by the Blair government, and the way that back gardens have shrunk to handkerchief size. Growing your own food is suddenly a radical act, just as it was when Collings was at the height of his campaigning powers. It is one in the eye for those who would prefer us to narrow our tastes to make us easier to process.

The process is far from over, and the battle far from won. Allotment sites are still being sold off by local authorities, though even more are still owned by railway companies or water companies. Some London councils sold them all in the 1980s, and the plots that remain are being sub-divided – which complicates the statistics.[43] But when reports suggested that the government was about to repeal the 1908 Act, there was outrage, campaigns announced by the *Independent on Sunday* – they called it 'Dig for Victory' – and a placatory statement by the Prime Minister.[44] Jesse Collings' campaign for smallholdings seems to be firmly off the agenda – though there are fringe debates about how to return the

---

[43] Greater London Assembly (2006), *A Lot to Lose: London's Disappearing Allotments*, London.
[44] Hansard (2011), 4 May.

population to agriculture – but his allotments campaign is growing in importance day by day.

The Back to the Land ideology remains unnamed and unacknowledged, but in the zeitgeist. Belief in the importance of allotments still goes hand in hand with an angry scepticism about the banking system, and about education that just prepares people to slot into dull, miserable and repetitive jobs. It goes hand in hand with the idea that we must redevelop the nation's real skills – *reskilling* as the Transition Towns movement calls it. Like the Distributists, the tradition is still in opposition to corporate power. Like Belloc and Chesterton, it identifies growing your own food as an assertion of liberty. Like Cobbett, it remains at the creative heart of self-help.

In fact, we increasingly – and despite the best efforts of those who rule us – see growing our own food, or even growing flowers, as a sign of economic and social health. When we see those flowerbeds at a railway station – rare these days – we see it as a sign that it is under the control of someone civilised, rather than a faceless corporate. But there are differences too. The movement is less melancholic than Chesterton. Thanks to think tanks like the New Economics Foundation, there are now ways forward that build allotments into workable blueprints for a future economy.

It is certainly less exclusively male. The key voices in the grow-your-own movement – from Rosie Boycott in London to Pam Warhurst in Todmorden – are now women. Those most likely to apply for allotments now are no longer retired men, but single parents, and often single mothers (one in three single mothers say they want an allotment).[45] Wander around the allotment space opposite my front door in Crystal Palace and you will see as many women as men working in their makeshift and productive environment, an amazing advertisement for informal solutions.

But the movement is also diverse in other ways too. There are Chinese plots, Jamaican plots, Portuguese plots, Irish plots, plots with plants from Palestine and the Caribbean, each one recognisable as distinctive, but knitted together by the same co-operative spirit – one of the best possible adverts for a multi-racial society and its benefits. The days when groups like English Array believed that going back to the land meant regenerating the English stock and English soil, protecting the Anglo-Saxon race, are no more. The open hospitality to outsiders that William Morris was at pains to portray in

---

[45] Hope and Ellis (2009), 12.

News from Nowhere is a feature of the allotments movement these days.[46] It probably always has been.

My own local allotments are full of characters from practically every culture on earth, yet they remain somehow deeply English – the Winnie-the-Poohs, the Rabbits and the Eeyores are all obvious. There are allotments nearly everywhere; even Mikhail Gorbachev encouraged them in the last days of the Soviet Union. There are allotments around the high rise flats of Bucharest just as there are around the cities of central America. Yet there is something deeply English about them in their individuality and practicality.

But behind all that, there is still an ideological message, borrowed from Cobbett, that small-scale, personal attention can be more productive than so-called 'economies of scale'. It poses the question about the spurious efficiencies of modern management: are we using the resources we have, human and agricultural, in the most effective way?

This is Andrew Simms, policy director of the New Economics Foundation, in 2007. "In 2004 the UK imported 17.2 million kilos of chocolate-covered waffles

---

[46] See study by Marcus Waithe (2006) *William Morris's utopia of strangers: Victorian medievalism and the ideal of hospitality*, Boydell & Brewer, Woodbridge.

and wafers and exported 17.6 million kilos; we imported 10.2 million kilos of milk and cream by weight, from France and exported 9.9 million," he wrote. "The figures for the same trade with Germany were 15.5 million kilos and 17.2 million. Germany sent us 1.5 million kilos of potatoes and we sent them, yes, 1.5 million kilos of potatoes. We imported 43,000 scarves from Canada and exported 39,000... Just as we imported 44,000 tonnes of frozen boneless cuts of chicken, we exported 51,000 tonnes of fresh boneless chicken. From an environmental perspective, it would seem that someone somewhere is pulling a chicken's leg."[47]

This is Jesse Collings almost exactly a century before:

"They say the land will not produce now. Has it lost its character? Take one article: how is it we buy every year £5,000,000 worth of cheese from the foreigner? Can England not produce this? How is it we purchase from £12,000,000 to £14,000,000 worth of butter? Is England not a butter producing country."[48]

---

[47] Andrew Simms, Dan Moran and Peter Chowla (2007) *UK Interdependence Report*, New Economics Foundation/Open University, London.
[48] Collings and Green (1920), 179.

That is a practical question and it is a political one too, and urgent in the face of that climate change-inducing trucking. We have the resources, the skills, the enthusiasm and the tradition of agriculture. Why have we allowed ourselves to be unemployed when we could feed ourselves and employ ourselves by producing our own, as we have for so many thousands of years before?

There is also something oddly modern about Gerald Butcher's paean of praise to allotments in 1918:

"Why do people love the land, yes, love it? Why are men land-hungry? Whence springs this craving for the indefinable, this peaceful satisfaction and intense enjoyment of the townsman working on his plot? Is it not in his blood? Is it not part of his nature, which many years of the artificial life of cities have been powerless, and always will be powerless, to subjugate? It needs only that the spark of the townsman's natural life be re-kindled, and his unbounded enthusiasm will burst into a flame of eager, earnest desire..."[49]

That rather overblown passage may also be a glimpse of the future. Food is a political issue that is increasingly

---

[49] Butcher (1918), 64-5.

potent. It isn't exactly land-hunger, which smacks of Hitlerian greed, but it certainly is nature hunger. It is something we all crave in different ways, some of us more than others of course, but all of us to some extent, whether it is for closer proximity to the shifts in seasons or for the feel of the earth between the fingers.

It is something we could all enjoy – if it wasn't for the houses in between.

Afterword

"If the old statute of Elizabeth, which laid down that every cottage built should have at least four acres of land attached to it, had been enforced until now, the land policy of this country and its relationship to the national food supply would be vastly different from what it is to-day; but we have to deal with things as they are..."
Gerald Butcher, *Allotments for All: The story of a great movement,* **1918**

This is not the first history of the allotments movement to be published in this country. It won't be the last either. Colin Ward and David Crouch wrote the classic history in 1988, but that is now nearly a quarter of a century ago and many things have changed since then. Most online allotment histories now are necessarily brief, and usually little more than lists of Parliamentary acts – without explaining the ferment of ideas and debate which lay behind them.

It is my contention that the allotments movement belongs to a lost political ideology, a half-forgotten political tradition in England, which has been driven underground by the Westminster elite. It is an ideology with a history that is sometimes proud, and sometimes less than proud, but which we need to be aware of as allotments and food production rises up the agenda.

That was why I wanted to write this history. It is personal and flawed as a result, but I hope it will provoke discussion on one side or the other. I also hope it will deepen our awareness of the tradition that lies behind the growth of allotments. But most of all, I hope it will revive the reputation of the man who did more for allotments in the UK than almost anybody else, whose memory has slowly dissipated in the nine decades since his death in 1920. That is why I start the story at a point which is really in the middle, but with the emergence of the great agrarian campaigner, Jesse Collings. For the more recent period, I've been enormously helped by conversation with Jack Dudley-Swale, though any mistakes and misinterpretations are all mine.

I can't pretend, just because I have written this book, that I am in any way expert in growing vegetables myself. I am married to someone who is, and have learned an immeasurable amount from Sarah, much of which has been used as compost for this short book. I have also had my life enriched by living down a dirt track in the middle of south London, and more particularly in the middle of the Spa Hill Allotments. That is why I dedicate this book to the Spa Hill Allotments Society and their members.

David Boyle, Crystal Palace, 2012